# The *Loneliest* Fall

*for those in search
of understanding*

*Kiana Moné*

 iUniverse®

THE LONELIEST FALL
FOR THOSE IN SEARCH OF UNDERSTANDING

iUniverse books may be ordered through booksellers or by contacting:

iUniverse
1663 Liberty Drive
Bloomington, IN 47403
www.iuniverse.com
844-349-9409

Because of the dynamic nature of the Internet, any web addresses or links contained in this book may have changed since publication and may no longer be valid. The views expressed in this work are solely those of the author and do not necessarily reflect the views of the publisher, and the publisher hereby disclaims any responsibility for them.

ISBN: 978-1-6632-0551-3 (sc)
ISBN: 978-1-6632-1320-4 (hc)
ISBN: 978-1-6632-0550-6 (e)

Library of Congress Control Number: 2020913145

Print information available on the last page.

iUniverse rev. date: 11/13/2020

# Introduction

My name is Kiana Monè, I'm 20 years old, and I write poetry. Let me start by giving you some background about me. I've been writing poems since I was 12 years old. I've always been passionate about poetry and how I could tell a story through it that other people could relate to.

I found myself falling in love with poetry as the years went by and I got older. I really leaned on poetry through all of the bad and good times I've had in my life. Poetry to me is a way to release the things in my heart and mind when I can't find the right words to say or that I am afraid to say. I've been passionate about a lot of things but nothing has ever even come close to this.

At first I was shy when sharing my poems with others because of how personal they are to me and for fear that other people wouldn't understand why I wrote the things I wrote or felt the way I felt, after all, a lot of my poems are written in my most fragile moments, but I realized that other people could use some of that fragileness in a time where it feels like everyone is taught to just be tough.

The truth is that we all have moments where we just want to feel like someone understands us. So I had an idea, I wanted to create a book of poems, my poems so that I could share my "stories" with people who have the same love for poetry as me. I am in a new chapter in my life and these poems are the past for me but to you, the reader, this will be your first time experiencing and reading about a chapter in my life that has closed. Either way, thank you for reading and trying to understand my journey.

I want you to know that no matter what you are going through you will never be alone in it as I have been through it too. Heartbreak, extreme sadness, healing, and love. You will come out on top and triumphant with a lesson every time. There is beauty in change and may we all be able to experience it in our lifetime.

# Note To My Readers

Some of these poems are not my own in the sense that I've drawn inspiration and pain from experiences I've listened to others speak about. Some of these poems came into my mind while I was doing things like listening to someone tell a story about a heartbreak they never thought they could get over, and some of these poems are about my own experiences with heartbreak.

Some of these poems were written at 3:00am when I couldn't sleep. Some of these poems were written in a bathroom. Some of these poems just popped into my head and I started writing. Some of these poems have made me cry. Some of these poems are not perfect. Some of these poems are unfinished, under nurtured, and simple.

Some of these poems are old and written in times where I was angry, lost, hurt, and confused. Some of these poems are dark and reek of depression. Some of these poems come from a place I never hope to revisit.

Some of these poems I'm not confident in, and some of these poems were written in the now where I am learning to grow and heal from things that I thought I would never get past. Some of these poems are about people who are no longer in my life and I just want to say that I have no ill feelings towards you, you are just simply apart of my story. I wish you well.

All of these poems are my truth and they are real. I hope my story is told the right way, I hope these poems are stories you can relate to, cry about, think about, understand, and heal with.

I hope this poem book gets into the right hands.

I hope as a reader you're not disappointed.

I hoped that you...

Enjoy.

# Heartbreak...

This is an unfamiliar pain, I think I am experiencing my first heartbreak.

# The loneliest fall

*Sometimes I wonder what it would*
*Be like if I never met you at all*
*Would I be happy?*
*And no I don't think my*
*Sadness is your fault*
*To it you just kind of added*
*I was broken long before I met you*
*And you were broken long*
*Before I met you too*
*And we figured that if we could*
*Hold each other tight enough*
*That we could put the pieces*
*Of our shattered hearts*
*Back together and they*
*Would become anew*
*But deep down we both knew*
*That pain doesn't work this way*
*And two hurt people can't heal*
*Each other yet here we are*
*Trying to heal one another*
*And I wish it didn't hurt so bad*
*Letting go of what I know*
*And I know we're not completely*
*Done but I feel my soul letting go*
*My eyes are getting tired from*
*Shedding heavy tears and*
*My heart has a weight on it*
*My mind is tired of running*
*Away from it, I asked God if*
*I should be with you but he*
*Never answers, or maybe I*
*Just don't want to hear because*

1

*I'm afraid that he'll tell me to*
*Move on when my heart wants*
*To stay, I just don't understand*
*Why it had to be you and me*
*Why we had to be the ones to*
*Let go of it all, now I'm hurting*
*In the silence of the loneliest fall*

### I only want you while it's storming

*I only want you while it's storming*
*Things like that seem to confuse most*
*But we understand*
*On a regular sunny day everything feels like*
*We force ourselves to be around each other*
*When we want to be out in the sun somewhere else*
*When it's storming I feel like we don't have a choice*
*But we don't really care to have a choice*
*Because the storm keeps us inside cuddling*
*Under each other*
*Maybe it's the fact that our hearts race*
*After every boom and crackle*
*And we can't even make each other feel that*
*Way on a regular day*
*Maybe it's the way it seems like the*
*Whole world stops and for a second it's just*
*The two of us*
*When usually we can't be bothered by*
*Each other's presence and we do our own things*
*This is the only time when something is louder*
*Than the sounds of us arguing*
*Sometimes when it rains I think God cries for us*
*He sees we don't deserve each other*
*So he gives us days like these to see*
*How truly lonely we are*
*Everything inside and outside of the house*
*Is making noise but us*
*We hold each other silently*
*With not a topic or word to speak to each other*
*Because we don't even know each other anymore*
*How could I be laying with you but feel so lonely*
*I'm empty but the storm keeps me holding onto you*

*And you holding on to me*
*And we just stay like that*
*Afraid to say what the other is thinking*
*As flickers of lights from lightning flashes in*
*I see how you feel within*
*You can't even hold it inside anymore*
*It's all over your skin*
*Your eyes can't even stare into mines anymore*
*I know the love is gone*
*We don't have to be with each other*
*But please just hold me while it storms*
*I only want you while it's storming*
*Because that's the only time you seem to want me*

## *I talked to God about you*

*I asked him if you were the one*
*I never hear him speak back to me*

## *Losing game*

*I was young & dumb*
*A fool in love*
*But love is a losing game*

## Love on a weighing scale

*We love on a weighing scale*
*Some things are too heavy to carry*
*Love and hate being two*
*If only we knew how to balance both*
*When one outweighs the other*
*We both know how far it can go*
*You tip the scale with the bass in your voice*
*And me with the roll of my eyes*

*Our tongues are so sharp*
*We don't need to sharpen our knives*
*But once the war is over*
*We slither back together*
*Like two sinful serpents and*
*Separate at the Weighing scale*
*You're on one side and I stand on the other*
*Today we are lovers*
*But tomorrow we will hate again*

*Which side will win?*
*We don't know but we can't go*
*Because without the other significant other*
*The scale will weigh uneven*
*And as if that is good reason*
*We decide to stay*

*Ask God for forgiveness*
*Because we have sinned away all that was left*
*And screamed away every last breath*
*If you stop fighting, I will too*
*If you stop lying, I will too*
*If your skeletons fall out of your closet*
*Mines will too*

*We are just two bodies*
*Folded and hunched over*
*Praying like origami folds*
*To stay on this weighing scale*
*Though we know*
*There might not be anything*
*Left to weigh*

## *Should I move on?*

*If I don't feel comfortable*
*Should I stay, stay with*
*Someone I'm not sure of?*
*Certain things that are said*
*Makes me wonder if I'm the*
*Only one, the lonely one*
*Certain things I see*
*Makes me wonder if*
*He really wants to be with me*

# Who are you?

*I wish you could see who you've become*
*I don't know you anymore*
*I used to think I did*
*But it's becoming clear that*
*I deserve more*
*No more excuses*
*It's all useless if you're not willing*
*To do right by me*
*Never asked you for a thing*
*But to love me*
*You put everything you could above me*
*And I cannot sacrifice my happiness*
*For you*
*I've grown up and you've stayed the same*
*And I cannot blame you for not wanting to change*
*But I cannot repeat cycles that I've*
*Been trying so hard to break*
*So I say goodbye*
*And I won't lie because it hurts*
*But I'll be in pain for the rest of my days*
*Before I let you steal my peace*
*This whole thing was just me being silly again*
*Thinking that you would understand my worth*
*But you don't have to understand*
*I'm not perfect but I love unapologetically*
*And that's something no one can take from me*
*Not even you*
*I wish I could say that nothing changed*
*I wish I could say that I trusted you to*
*Or that we just grew apart*
*But I know I don't believe that in my heart*
*You change like the seasons*

*I will not **fall** for it again*
*I thought that love could fix it*
*But it can't fix this part*
*Love cannot change the fact that*
*I no longer know who you are*

## *Fix it*

*I don't know how to fix it*
*But I can't erase this feeling*
*Even though I wish I could*

## *Where did you go?*

*Where did you go?*
*I wanted you standing right*
*Next to me*
*But now you're gone for good*
*And it's really gotten the best of me*
*Now I'm opening up*
*And spilling out the rest of me*
*Where did you go?*
*I wanted you standing right next*
*To me*

## *To Trust*

*Finally admitted to myself*
*That I'm afraid to trust*
*It's not that I'm scared of love*
*I'm just scared of lies*
*Someone selling me dreams*
*While looking into my eyes*
*Someone pretending to be*
*A lover or friend*
*Only to really hurt me in the end*
*Everyone says I think too negative*
*They say I have to learn to trust*
*But the truth is that*
*My minds all messed up*
*I've been stabbed in the back*
*By people I loved*

# Most people fear love

Most people fear love
I fear it doesn't exist
Look how we fall out of love
And fall into hate so quick
Love is supposed to be infinite
When you love someone
You're supposed to mean it
You're supposed to show it
You're supposed to say it
I fear that because I don't
Believe in it I won't know
How to reciprocate it
Most people fear love
Because they don't want
Their hearts broken
I fear it because love
Will have me open
Open to fake love
Open to hate
Sometimes I get on
My knees and pray
To remember how to love
Because sometimes I forget
And sometimes I say hurtful shit
Sometimes I don't know if I love
Anyone at all and I fear that
I don't even love myself
But what is a world without love?
Is it hell?
But what if love is hell?
What if it burns me?
What if love hurts every thought

*I have in my mind?*
*Why should I allow myself to get hurt?*
*Why should I take a chance with my heart?*
*I fear that I'll love you more than I love myself*
*And that is the ultimate hell*
*That is the scariest part*

## In a perfect world

*In a perfect world*
*I could trust the ones I love*
*I could trust that they would love me back*
*In the way that I need to be loved*
*In a perfect world I wouldn't have*
*Fucked up trust*
*I wouldn't have to question everyone I love*
*I'm all messed up*
*And I'm not blaming anyone for the way I am*
*Because I am the reason*
*Trusting and believing*
*That everything that glitters would be gold*
*But we all know that gold ain't glitter*

## *Untitled 1*

*I feel empty inside but yet*
*I'm still trying to love you*
*I've left pieces of me on marble floors*
*Pieces of me that are battered and bruised*
*I've left my heart on my sleeve*
*Until there was no more of me*
*Only you and more of you*
*I am incapable of love*
*But without love what will I do?*

## Memories

*Memories keep pieces of you with me*
*Pieces I've been trying to leave behind*
*And memories of you constantly*
*Dance around my mind*
*Most times I wish the memories would die*
*But then a piece of me would go with them*
*I often think a lot about love*
*But I don't think you truly loved me*
*Or maybe you just couldn't love me*
*In the way that I need*
*Because if you really loved me*
*Why was it so easy to leave?*
*I tell myself*
*It doesn't matter*
*And the truth is that it doesn't*
*It was what it was*
*And it wasn't what it wasn't*
*I can't force my love on you*
*Or make you feel the same way I do*
*But I just wish you could understand how*
*It feels*
*To love someone who is here and there*
*But never where you need them to be*
*To love someone who is unsure of you*
*I guess you don't know what you meant to me*
*Once again the past is the past*
*And I'm at peace with the situation now*
*Sometimes I just wish that the memories*
*Would see their way out*
*Out of my mind*
*And my personal space*

*My heart has moved on*
*But my mind is stuck in place*
*Still making up scenarios about you and me*
*Refusing to give up on the memories*

## Pride

*I know I have too much pride*
*But I don't want to expose my true side*
*I don't want to be open to pain*
*I've opened up and i've had nothing to gain*
*I've opened up and I still felt the same*
*And opening up did not make you stay*
*I let my pride get the best of me sometimes*
*But I don't want to cry*
*And I don't see why I have to apologize*
*When no one has to me*
*No one has given me closure*
*And i've been messed over so many times*
*And I won't lie*
*No matter how hard I try*
*My pride just won't die*

### Do you want to hear a joke?

*How many times do you find love in a lifetime?*
*Trick question*
*The answer is none*

# *Fuck love*

*Fuck you!*
*But I love you*
*Can't seem to put anyone*
*Else above you*
*Love is crazy*
*It makes you do some crazy*
*Shit and maybe*
*That's why I keep legit*
*Doing crazy shit*
*Do you love me?*
*Because if you don't then*
*Leave me alone*
*But you, I just can't seem to forget*
*I'm good on my own*
*But I'd rather be with you*
*And that's the honest fucking truth*
*But I'm not about*
*To chase you*
*I've done that enough*
*You don't love anybody but yourself*
*And that's why I can't trust you*
*Fuck you!*
*Yeah I said it again*
*You can't keep playing with my heart*
*Just so you can break it again*
*I'm not made of stone nigga*
*My heart ain't that strong nigga*
*Do you not know where you belong nigga?*
*I'm tired of being With you*
*But still feeling alone*
*Just leave me alone*
*You know you're wrong*

**23**

*And I don't want anything else*
*To do with you*
*So while I'm at it*
*Fuck love*
*And fuck you too!*

# *I'm done*

*I don't care about love anymore*
*And I wish I never did in the first place*
*Love ain't never did a thing for me*
*but cause heartbreak*
*I don't care about trust anymore*
*I ain't never trusted a soul*
*I tried and I tried*
*But each time that i've trusted*
*I've always been proved wrong*

### I can't even say that it hurt

*I can't even say that it hurt*
*I'm used to the disappointment*
*What a shame...*
*I knew I fell out of love*
*When you wanted to go*
*And I didn't care if you stayed*

## Falling out of love

*I think I'm falling*
*Out of love with you*
*I don't see the same*
*Things I used to see*
*You've put everything you*
*Possibly could above me*
*And even when you didn't*
*Have a thing, I was there*
*For you and I cared for you*
*But no matter how much*
*You love someone you can't*
*Make them love you too*
*I tell myself it's better to let go*
*But it just isn't that easy*
*I tell myself to forget about it*
*But my heart keeps telling*
*Me that you need me*
*And honestly I used to think*
*I needed you*
*But now that I know that's not*
*True, I find it harder to stay*
*With someone that doesn't*
*Know if I'm worth the fight*
*I guess everybody was right*
*And that's what I hate the most*
*I wanted it to be you and me*
*But I guess that isn't how it goes*
*And if you can't see what you*
*Mean to me, no matter how much*
*I show it, then when you read this*
*I'm sure you'll know it*
*My heart is starting to let go of you*

*There's nothing else I can do*
*It used to be you I could trust*
*But my heart has had enough*
*And though I still care about you*
*I'm falling out of love*

## *Trigger fingers*

*You got trigger fingers*
*You shot me down*
*You took me high*
*And then you watched me drown*
*Then the bullet struck*
*And you watched me bleed out*
*I don't think you cared even a drop*
*About how it made me feel*
*To keep it real*
*I think you just liked the sound*

## *Emotions*

*Love is like a battlefield*
*A raging war that I can't win*
*And so I throw in the towel*
*I say truce*
*I have a hard time with emotions*
*I'm afraid of being used*
*I make dumb decisions*
*Feelings clouding my better judgement*
*Please don't judge me*
*I'm just young and I fuck up*
*I tell myself I better toughen up*
*Because feelings leave you soft*
*Next thing you know*
*The other significant other's feelings fade*
*And now you're lost*
*And then you say "it's their loss"*
*But what did they really lose anyway*
*What is the point of love anyways*
*What is the point of anything these days?*
*If everything is temporary*

# *Untitled 2*

*Her heart speaks of everything*
*under the sun*
*Emptiness ain't so fun*
*When you're in love alone*
*Hearts used to be home*
*But now all their used for is malice*
*And practice for people who can't seem*
*To grasp the concept of love*
*Love is unconditional*
*But love these days comes with nothing*
*But conditions*
*And wishing that maybe a person*
*Would change*
*Even though you know that they're still the same*
*You keep chasing*
*When there's no one to catch*
*You keep loving and getting no love back*
*And ain't no pain like giving your all*
*But constantly being reminded*
*That's it's not enough*
*And even if it was it will never be*
*You can't satisfy someone*
*that will never see*
*And it's not your fault*
*It's human nature to want love*
*Even when you don't love yourself*

## The price we pay for love

*I paid the price for loving you*
*I paid the price for trusting you too*
*You've never cared about hurting me*
*And still I have forgiven you*
*I've charged the trust issues*
*You've caused me to the game*
*Because after all,*
*I am the only one to blame*
*Putting up with things I knew*
*I didn't deserve*
*Hoping that you'd change*

## Rewind

*If I could rewind back to the day we met*
*I would probably do it all over again*
*I would've kept things strictly as friends*
*Because now everything's a confusing mess*
*And my feelings are caught up in it*
*You're telling me one thing*
*But your actions are showing another*
*I used to think that we were each other's*
*Missing piece*
*But now that vision is getting so hard to see*
*Things used to be beautiful and bitter sweet*
*Now things are just complicated*
*I'm starting to feel jaded*
*I'm starting to feel the need to be alone*
*I'm starting to feel like you don't care*
*As long as you get what you want*
*You say you care but do you really?*
*I'm used to people playing mind games*
*So I can't fall for the tricks*
*I used to feel like you were all for this*
*But I know that feelings change*
*Mine have too*
*I wish I could rewind*
*Now that I know what this has come to*

## Closure

(For you.)

I need closure from something
That I'm not sure was something
In the first place
I've made some dumb mistakes
This probably being one of them
I thought that maybe you were my
Soulmate
But the timing is all wrong
You have unfinished baggage
That you're still carrying on
I still have unspoken sadness that
I have not taken steps to address
But damn does it suck to let go
But what am I letting go of
If you were never mine In the first place?
I've never felt like this about
Someone else
A spiritual connection
Some sort of bond created by God
Or an alignment of stars or something
You told me not to change on you
But you changed on me
And even after that I'm still not mad
Just disappointed that I trusted you
With parts of me that are fragile
Everything was wrong
But we tried to make it right
And in the end
We paid for it

*I wonder if your feelings were ever real*
*Or if I was just being a hopeless romantic again*
*I still don't understand what me & you had*
*I just know that it was reckless*
*It was beautiful*
*And then it was a wreck*
*It started & then it was over*
*We both needed closure*
*But I still wish it wasn't over*

## *Regret*

*I hope you regret*
*Fumbling my heart*
*When i've done nothing but*
*Love you from the very start*
*I wish that we would've just stayed friends*
*Because now we have to be strangers again*

# Sadness...

*I feel like sadness and grief have*
*attached themselves to me.*

# *A lot of things to say*

*I got a lot of things to say*
*But I don't say much*
*Or enough*
*If I say anything at all*

# *So far so good*

*So far so good*
*If good was good enough*
*But i'm me*
*So..*
*Good is never GREAT enough*
*Wish I wasn't so critical*
*Wish I wasn't so pitiful*

## *Hurt*

*"You better let that hurt go girl" they say*
*But hurt won't let me go these days*

## *Alone*

*I want to be alone*
*Not just right now but for good*
*I don't want to be bothered*
*Or provoked*
*I just want the world to leave me alone*
*I am tired of giving my all*
*And getting nothing in return*
*I am tired of showing love and in the end*
*Getting burned*
*I don't want to be negative or pessimistic*
*But right now I don't really care*
*Im hurt*

### Thank you for being there

*"Thank you for being there for me"*
*They say as I watch them*
*Walk right out of my life for good*
*Right when I need them*
*I'm always giving and never take*
*I wonder when someone will give to me*
*And never take*
*I'm tired of being the emotional crutch*
*When will I be enough for someone?*
*I'm tired of feeling temporary*
*And disposable but that's all I know*
*I only matter when someone needs me*
*But once they don't I'm like a ghost*
*Of the past*
*I'm not perfect*
*I do wrong too*
*But my intentions are never to do bad*
*I just want to feel like enough*
*And not just half of something*
*I want someone to fully care*
*I don't want to be used*
*And bruised*
*And battered up*
*I want to be loved*
*So much that people want to stay*
*Without me having to beg*
*Or pretend that it doesn't hurt*
*Because it does so bad*
*And life feels so unfair*
*And after I've given my all*
*Spilled out my soul*
*Destroyed myself*

*All I'm left with is someone telling me*
*"Thank you for being there"*
*As I watch them walk right*
*Out of my life*
*For good*
*Right when I need them.*

## Will you stay?

*If I tell you who I am you*
*Might not like who I am*
*And that's all I have*
*I'd hate to see you go*
*Because I'm not who*
*You thought I was*
*I'm not perfect*
*I'm a sad soul*
*A mad soul*
*A glad soul*
*I'm everything*
*That would scare*
*A person away*
*But still you stay*
*But you don't quite*
*Know the real me yet*
*And I figure that's why*
*You remain*
*But if I tell you who I am*
*You might not like who I am*
*And that's all I have*
*I've been more depressed*
*Than I've been glad*
*I've been less happy*
*And I've been more sad*
*And I don't want you*
*To have to carry my*
*Overflowed bags*
*When you have bags of*
*Your own*
*I know*
*I confuse you*

*But that's because I'm*
*Confused myself*
*Even if I wanted to*
*I couldn't help myself*

## Ever enough

I shared my soul with people
Who are empty
I poured myself into empty cups
Trying to love and be loved
By people who saw me as temporary
There is nothing temporary about me
I've never done anything without purpose
I've never done anything with ill intent
I've only loved with my whole heart
I've only tried to hear people out
But nothing is ever enough
Someone will always find a flaw
In me
Even when I attempt to be perfect
Even when I do everything right
But I'm tired of arguing
I don't have it in me to fight
I want more than what I've been given
I see the bigger picture of life
I'm not tied down to just physical attraction
I need to know what's in your mind
I need to know what's in your heart
When is how I feel going to matter?
When is someone going to step up
And fight for me?
I'm always doing all the fighting
And I'd be lying if I said I wasn't tired
If it was up to me I wouldn't love at all
I wouldn't feel at all
Sometimes I don't feel at all
I'm tired of patching things up
For them to unravel again
Because nothing is EVER enough

# I unravel

*I listen to my heart beat*
*Like snare drums*
*Loud enough to drown*
*Out the sounds of sorrow*
*Embedded in the deepest*
*Parts of my soul*
*And only heaven knows*
*If I'll get through it this time*
*It feels like this life of mine*
*Is on a repeat*
*I have lost a lot of things*
*And among those things*
*Was peace*
*I wonder if I'll ever be me again*
*Or if sadness has just attached*
*Itself to me*
*Sometimes happiness feels*
*Like it's a lifetime away*
*And sometimes it feels like*
*I'll never see better days*
*But I hope for my sake*
*Everything will be ok*
*I wonder what it's like to heal*
*I feel like I've been sewn up*
*But I unravel again and again*
*These are the thoughts*
*That reside In my mind*
*But I cannot bring my mouth to say*
*I have no tears left to cry*

### *Has anybody got the cure to sadness?*

*Has anybody got the cure to sadness?*
*For years there's been madness in my heart*
*There's been battles in the dark*
*Between me and my pillows*
*Even the weeping willows will cry over this*
*Hand over heart*
*But I am not praying to any flag*
*I am making sure it is still beating*
*It's so quiet sometimes*
*That it's loud and defeating*
*But I still have to make sure it's there*
*This is sorrow*
*So I ask God to please let me borrow*
*some happiness*
*Before I am swallowed by the sadness*
*Of tomorrow*
*Again and again*
*Please someone help me find the cure*

### Nowhere fast

*I'm going nowhere fast*
*Do you know where I can*
*Slow down?*
*I might just be going crazy*
*been feeling a little bit hazy*
*I've been moving at the speed*
*Of light*
*I've been battling with my mind*
*Everyone thinks I'm alright*
*And I thought I was fine*
*Until my thoughts poured in*
*At night*
*I said I just want to feel alright*
*I don't want to worry you*
*So I hold it all in*
*But when will I explode?*
*I don't know*
*Hopefully I won't*
*But some days it's hard*
*To be strong*
*I try to be a light in everyone's life*
*But I'm sitting in my own dark*
*Still I don't want to self pity*
*If I'm not what you expected*
*Please forgive me*
*I'm not like this all the time*
*I'm just like this often*
*I'm trying to get better*
*I'm taking it one day at a time*
*Trying to make sense of this life*
*I've been living with no destination*
*I have been struggling with changes*

*I don't know how long this will last*
*Or how long it will take to pass*
*Everyone asks me where I'm going*
*I'm going nowhere fast*

## Chaos

*This feeling has been weighing on me*
*So heavy that I don't know if I can shake it*
*I feel like my body is not my own*
*My heart is not my own*
*And my mind is my only home*
*I stay inside my head so much that*
*I wonder if I've ever been outside of it*
*I never genuinely feel satisfied*
*Or happy with life*
*And I hate it because I'm blessed*
*To be alive*
*I'm at a point where I am numb*
*And I feel no pain*
*Just disappointed*
*And drained*
*I know that people are counting on me*
*And so I'm ashamed*
*All I can think of is negative things*
*I'm afraid of the unknown*
*Crippled with anxiety and fear*
*I wish that I didn't feel so deep*
*I wish that I could just brush off things*
*But I'm like a human sponge*
*Soaking things in*
*Until I'm squeezed out and there's*
*Nothing left inside*

# My Mind

*They don't understand my mind*
*And why I am the way I am*
*But I can't explain why I turned*
*Out the way that I did*
*I think so deep and I feel even deeper*
*Everyone's on the outside*
*Looking in*

# Nagging feeling

*Here comes this nagging feeling again*
*That feeling that never truly seems to go away*
*A voice in the back of my head that says*
*That nothing will ever change*
*Some days I'm fine*
*Some days I'm not sure how I feel at all*
*Some days I want to sleep all day*
*And some days I barely sleep at all*
*I'm not sure what I'm feeling*
*I just know that it doesn't feel good*
*Or right*
*But still when I'm asked how I'm doing*
*I say I'm doing fine*
*I'm not sure if that's the truth or a lie*
*Things haven't really been "normal"*
*For a really long time*
*It's kind of numbing when you've*
*Been ignoring your feelings for so long*
*That you don't even know*
*If your feelings are your own*
*Sometimes I can be a sponge*
*I absorb the feelings of others*
*To make up for my feelings*
*Or the lack thereof*
*Sometimes my heart beats fast for*
*No reason*
*And I listen to it beating*
*Sometimes it's so quiet that it's defeating*
*Sometimes life feels like a series*
*Of mistakes*
*A series of unfortunate events*
*A series of unspoken pain*

*I write out the things I feel*
*Because it's harder to say*
*It's hard to look someone in the face*
*And tell them you're not ok*
*I don't want to discuss why I feel this way*
*Because I don't really know*
*And I don't want to burden anyone*
*With my problems when they all*
*Have their own*
*I constantly overthink*
*I feel bad for doing what's best for me*
*I think people are thinking things that*
*They probably don't even think*
*I need too much reassurance*
*Sometimes I feel useless*
*And all of this is stupid but it's the truth*
*I can feel it tapping me on the shoulder*
*The nagging feeling has just re begun*
*And it's far from being over*

## I just wanna be

*I just wanna be happy*
*I'm tired of feeling broken*
*Tell me what I have to do*
*I cannot be open*

## God Please

*God please help me*
*I've been crying out to you*
*My mind is driving me crazy*
*And I don't know what to do*
*I haven't been myself lately*
*And no one has a clue*
*But I can't blame them*
*Because I haven't told the truth*
*I've been telling everyone*
*That i'm ok*
*But I feel i'm going insane*
*I can't stop thinking*
*Wish I could numb the pain*

## *Tired*

*I am tired*
*I am exhausted*
*If I could sleep*
*Then maybe i'd be ok*
*I've been dealing with*
*Inner turmoil*
*From a very young age*
*And year after year*
*Things just add on*
*To the pain*
*Sometimes i'm numb*
*And sometimes I feel*
*Everything all the same*

## Through the motions

*I just be going through the motions*
*There's no rhyme or reason*
*Nothing is steady*
*Everything constantly changes*
*Like the seasons*
*I won't let myself get used to anything*
*Because it's bound to change*
*And I don't want to get comfortable*
*If things won't stay the same*
*I know life is all about growth*
*Making mistakes and also pain*
*I know that life can be joyful*
*But I'm always expecting of rain*
*Sometimes I do things that I don't understand*
*But lately I haven't been caring at all*
*I guess I'm just over life*
*Haven't really cared about doing things right*
*I'm just going through the motions*
*I barely feel emotions*
*I rarely deal with emotions*
*I'd rather hold everything in*
*Than spill my soul out to other souls*
*Who don't really care*
*Or maybe they do*
*And I'm just pessimistic*
*Always thinking that I'm being used*
*It's not far fetched*
*Everyone's always out for something*
*I don't think one person has really cared*
*About me at all*
*And I'm talking about the real me*
*Not just my looks or physicality*

*I'm talking about the real me*
*The fucked up me*
*The me that's deep down*
*Sensitive*
*Soft spoken*
*Easily hurt*
*Used*
*And so broken*
*I can't sleep*
*But I won't get too deep*
*Because I hate talking about emotions*
*This feels never ending*
*So I'm just going through the motions*

## *Maybe*

*I don't know who I am anymore*
*Sometimes I wonder if I ever*
*Really knew who I was at all*
*Or maybe I've always been this way*

## E.A.N.A.A.

*I sometimes feel like everything*
*And nothing at all*
*Like sometimes I feel everything*
*And other times I feel nothing at all*

## Deadly thinking

*I overthink my way out of things*
*That could be good for me*
*I think people are thinking things*
*That they wouldn't be*
*I don't care what people say*
*But my mind says that's a lie*
*And so I care*
*And i'm aware that it's all just thoughts*
*But I can't stop thinking*
*I over analyze my life*
*And the people in it*

### ???

*What the fuck am I doing?*
*I feel stuck on stupid*
*Always fucking up*
*Shit always gets ruined*

## The point is?

*What's the point?*
*Of anything*
*Of everything*
*What's the point of showing love*
*If your heart is only going to*
*Get shattered*
*What's the point of trusting*
*When someone will always lie*
*What's the point of living*
*When in the end we all die*
*What's the point?*
*Of anything*
*Of everything*
*In this moment I don't feel a thing*
*I said everything that I could say*
*I've cried every tear that I could cry*
*And still nothing has changed*
*I am tired of being the lonely one*
*Is anyone really ever the only one?*
*I don't think so*
*But all I know is that I just don't*
*Have it in me to care anymore*
*Because what's the point?*

## My happy poem

*Wish I could write a happy poem*
*But I'd have to be happy to do that*
*Seems like I've been less happy*
*And more sad*

## *"Free me"*

*Please free me from the negative*
*Energy that keeps me hanging*
*By a thread*
*Please free me from the no good*
*Voices in my head*
*When I lay down,*
*I'd rather lay down In peace instead*
*Please free me from sadness and sorrow*
*Because tomorrow I want to feel good*
*Please tell me that everything I'm telling you*
*Is understood*
*Because I can't afford another disappointment*

# A sad day

*Sad days are the hardest*
*On these days I find it the*
*Hardest to smile & put on*
*A poker face, on these days*
*I want to hide so the world*
*Doesn't see me cry & wash*
*My pride away*
*On these days I wish I didn't*
*Wake up at all & maybe my*
*Problems wouldn't seem so tall*

## *Idk*

*Outer space*
*Out of time*
*I have been living*
*Like I want to die*
*And the people*
*They all wonder why*
*I don't have an answer*
*So I won't lie*
*I've been going through it*
*Can you see it in my eyes*
*I have lost it*
*I stumbled out my mind*
*I say please help me*
*I haven't been myself*
*They can't help me I can't*
*Help myself*
*I just want to be alright*
*I just want to sleep through the night*
*I am praying*
*Maybe I'm not praying right*
*Just hold me*
*I don't want to be alone*
*Please wake me*
*When everything's not wrong*
*I keep going*
*In this life you have to be strong*
*Though I wonder*
*For exactly how long*
*Outer space*
*Out of time*
*I have been living*
*Like I want to die*

*And the people*
*They all wonder why*
*I don't have an answer*
*So I won't lie*

## *So they say*

*They tell me the sun will shine again*
*But when?*
*I have nothing left to give*

## Silly me

*Silly me*
*Listening to my heart skip beats again*
*As I lay in my dark room*
*The clock says it's a quarter past ten*
*A quarter too late, I should've went to sleep*
*Long ago*
*Because now I've left room for my mind to roam*
*Silly me*
*I think about everything I've ever done*
*All the things I'm not proud of*
*All the things I should've said*
*But now will be burned into my mind*
*Like a catchy theme song*
*And I'll sing along every night if I allow myself*
*Silly me*
*I cried tonight*
*I laid down in a bed of lies tonight*
*Told to me by myself*
*And I'll listen to them all*
*Because I believe their right*
*Silly me*
*I asked God if he would sit with me*
*Sometimes I'm afraid of the thoughts*
*The night provokes*
*I prayed away every sin*
*Though I will sin again*
*And lie in the same sad position*
*Tomorrow night*
*Silly me*
*I closed my eyes*
*My heart feels heavy sometimes*
*It keeps me awake some nights*

*But I don't want to worry the stars*
*So I lay under them silently*
*Listening to my heart beat quietly*
*Silly me*
*I won't wake up feeling the same way*
*As the day has brought in new feelings*
*And the sun has brought me a new healing*
*Before I have to face the night again*
*Silly me*

### Hello, my name is depression

*My name is depression*
*And i'm pretty sly*
*I'll sneak up when you're happy*
*And make you wish you would die*
*I could ruin your happiness in the*
*Blink of an eye*
*The only thing I need to do*
*Is fill up your mind*
*I will make you feel everything*
*I'll let you get up really high*
*Then take you down really low*
*I'll make you bury your emotions*
*Until you want to explode*
*I'll snatch a smile off your face*
*And make you go through hell*
*I know you won't tell*
*Because you don't want to be judged*
*You will never get enough of me*
*I am your only drug*
*You'll never really have anyone*
*Because I won't allow you to trust*
*I'll fill your head with bad thoughts*
*Because you don't deserve love*
*I'll push you to the edge*
*And tell you to jump*
*I'll say "do it" and you will*
*Hello, my name is depression*
*And I like to kill*

## *Nothingness*

*I don't feel anything*
*But I feel everything*
*If that even makes sense*
*I've been chasing a feeling*
*That I'm starting to believe*
*Doesn't even exist*
*I find myself wandering and wondering*
*"What's the point of anything"*
*There are many things that*
*I wish were different*
*But everything is constantly*
*The same*
*Nothing has changed*
*Except for me*
*I don't know who I am*
*I don't even remember who I*
*Used to be*
*I thought I had a clue*
*But then something happens*
*Out of the blue*
*That reminds me that I still*
*Don't know*
*I start to think about life*
*And how I'm always battling my*
*Mind*
*But even I get tired*
*And I'd be a liar if I said I didn't*
*I don't want to die*
*But I don't care to be alive*
*And I'm sorry but that is my truth*
*This may come as a surprise*
*As I always keep a good poker face*

*But it's getting harder and harder*
*To pretend that I'm ok*
*I feel complete nothingness*
*Emptiness*
*Like I have nothing left to give*
*Yet and still I feel*
*I wish I could be still*
*Still I pray that the nothingness*
*Will go away*

## Untitled 3

*I'm starting to feel numb again*
*I hate the feeling of nothingness*

## Numb

*I'm starting to be numb*
*I'm starting to forget how to feel*
*People come and they go*
*I don't question things anymore*
*I know that nothing is real*
*Everyone is here for a moment*
*And then they're gone*
*And I'm still here by myself*
*I'm starting to be numb*
*I'm who everyone comes*
*To talk to*
*But I have no one to talk to*
*Not that I want to anyways*
*It's a shame*
*I never used to be this way*
*Now I know no other way*
*I give my all*
*I get nothing in return*
*I do everything right*
*Yet and still nothing is right*
*Now I don't want to try*
*I'm all burned out*
*A mess*
*Shit ain't been normal*
*In a long while*
*I've always been depressed*
*Shit been eating me up*
*But I'm not going to say*
*A thing*
*Ain't nothing anyone*
*Can do to help*
*I've accepted myself*

*I'm not the same anymore*
*And it can't be changed*
*Or reversed*
*I feel I've been cursed*
*I won't make it worse by*
*Continuing to open up*
*I've had enough*
*I'd rather be numb*

## Self care

*I ain't been caring about self lately*
*I've been self pitying*
*Been venting to myself and maybe*
*It ain't the best thing to do*
*But what else is there to do*
*When you haven't been feeling*
*Like yourself lately*
*I ain't been caring about self lately*
*I've been ignoring my problems*
*Letting them pile up*
*Until I can't take it and maybe*
*It ain't the best thing to do*
*But what else is there to do*
*When you haven't been feeling*
*Like yourself lately*
*I ain't been caring about self lately*
*I get up and make myself up*
*But I can't make this up*
*I've been numb*
*And still I ain't been caring*
*About self lately*

## The ugly truth

*I wish I could say I was happy*
*And mean it too*
*I wish I could say I was at peace*
*But I'd be lying to you*
*Nothing about this has been easy at all*
*It has been way too hard to stand*
*And much more easy to fall*
*I've been fighting for my life*
*Because I don't want to die*
*But sometimes I don't feel like*
*I have the will to live*
*But I don't want to burden the ones*
*I care about with my pain*
*I must be insane*
*Pretending to be sane*
*When I'm hurting like this*

## Pitch Black

*I lay in the pitch black*
*On my back*
*With my hands slumped over my chest*
*As I breathe air in and out of my lungs*
*My eyes closed*
*With tears streaming down my face*
*As I lay still & silent*
*Right now*
*It feels like I am the only person*
*In the world who feels like this*
*Though I know there are others*
*Somewhere else in the world feeling*
*Just like this*
*Lying in the same position*
*The pitch black is lonely*
*But it's the only place I can be myself*
*It's the only place where I can't hide*
*From myself*
*My heart consumes my body*
*And my mind brings every thought to life*
*That I've tried so hard to bury*
*All of my mistakes*
*All of my pain*
*All of the times that I couldn't get*
*something right*
*I lay in the pitch black until the sun rises*
*The next day and swallows the night*
*But even then I won't get up*
*Until my body says that it's ok*
*Sometimes it's never ok*
*But I force myself to get up*
*And keep moving anyways*

*But most days*
*I don't want to get up*
*Most days I'd rather lay in the*
*Pitch black*
*Most days I want to give up*
*I'm scared that one day the pitch black*
*Will swallow me up*
*Before the sun rises*
*The next day*

## No peace

*I can't get no peace*
*I can't even sleep*
*I can't trust nobody*
*I can't even trust me*
*So much shit to drown in*
*Feels like I'm 6 ft deep*
*And I don't even feel like*
*Digging my way out*
*I've had enough of fake love*
*And people using me*
*People smiling in my face*
*I feel like I'm losing me*
*I've been strong for so long*
*That I don't know how to be weak*
*All that I know is I can't get no peace*
*Who do you call*
*When your backs against the wall*
*And nobody can understand*
*I try to lean on God*
*But I don't even have the strength*
*To get on my knees and pray*
*I'm not suicidal and I don't want to die*
*But I think about it from time to time*
*I don't see a future*
*I'm just taking it day by day*
*Y'all want me to be honest*
*But my honest isn't pretty*
*My honest isn't roses and daisies*
*My honest is gloomy and hazy*
*My honest is depressing*
*But it's hard to change*
*Y'all want me to be open*

*But I don't have it in me*
*I think I've been quiet for so long*
*That I'm running empty*
*I'm scared and angry*
*Sad and anxiety*
*Depressed and stressed*
*But I know that I'm blessed*
*So I keep holding on*
*So I keep on*
*I keep on*

## The weight of the WORLD

Sometimes the weight of the world
Is too heavy of a burden to carry
So I turn my lights out and lay in the dark
Weariness grows steadily on my heart
Dreams seem far and light years away
At times like this I get on my knees and pray
Prayers that heal the parts of my heart
That I am not brave enough to face
And all I need to do is let go
But it's hard to let go if all you know is
How to stay the same
But I want to change and learn to be
More grateful for the air that I breathe
Even if my 24 hours was not the 24 hours
I had hoped for
I hope for more sunny days
That will break through the pain
And though all scars do not erase
I pray that hope will always remain
I may not have it all
Or be where I want to be
But I know
Time will set me free

## Lost ones

(For Stephen)

*Please give me guidance*
*For I am lost without you*
*I am no time keeper but*
*I know you're gone to soon*
*I pray for those that have*
*been lost like I lost you*
*I don't know where you've*
*Gone but I hope you're where*
*I think you are, wherever you*
*Have went I hope your love*
*Is not far, because loss is hard*
*But I cannot make you stay*
*And I cannot replay the days*
*But I can still replay the pain*
*And all the same scars still*
*Remain, I pray that my vision*
*Of you never fade, I hope*
*People who have lost like me*
*Stay strong and I hope the*
*People who are lost like you*
*Eventually make it home.*

## Sonder

*I wonder if the passerby's*
*Think about what my life is like*
*I wonder if they wonder about*
*A mind like mines*
*I wonder where they come from*
*Stories in their eyes*
*And their stories may be stories*
*More complex than mines*
*I wonder about their pain*
*Their disappointments and their mistakes*
*I wonder if they all wonder the same*
*I often think about life and the passerby*
*How we all live in a world*
*But a world not intertwined*
*How I'll see someone that I'll never see again*
*Passing me in a car or walking by*
*And there's so many people*
*In the world that I'll never meet*
*But they all matter so much to someone else*
*Their all loved by someone else*
*Missed by someone else*
*But have no connection to me*
*It's a mysterious world that we live in*
*And we are all just pieces to a larger puzzle*
*I wonder if the passerby*
*Wonders why*
*I think of them*

### *Where do the confused souls go?*

*I've always wondered where the confused souls go*
*The ones whose life's we're not fulfilled*
*Whose dreams were put on hold*
*What happened to those people who lives were cut short*
*But they were not ready to leave*
*The fallen whose voices are blowing in the wind*
*Through the trees*
*What happened to the souls who are between*
*Life and death?*
*The ones who are gone but never really left*
*The souls who were misunderstood*
*And now they are wrecked*
*The ones that have gone and wished us all the best*
*The ones whose smiles will never be put to rest*
*The happiness that has been stolen*
*But never really been put to death*
*I guess the question in this poem is do they*
*Really leave everything behind?*
*Or do the lost, clueless, and confused souls*
*Find their way back from time to time?*

## Gone far away

(For Stephen)

*Sometimes I like to think of it*
*As a permanent vacation*
*Just to take the edge off a little*
*The words gone forever effects*
*Me in ways the world does not know*
*Ways I don't show but sometimes*
*I break down when I'm alone*
*Sometimes my heart feels cold*
*And I feel numb because*
*I've never fully healed from this*
*I think of things I should've, could've said*
*And things I could've did*
*It hurts even more that no matter*
*What I couldn't have prevented it*
*I wonder if you've met God*
*I wonder if the angels took you in*
*I wonder if you know what heaven is like*
*Or if you watch me from time to time*
*I wonder if you know how much I love you*
*and how broken I feel without you*
*I always know a piece is missing*
*And I know that it's you*
*I wonder if you miss living*
*Just as much as I miss you breathing*
*and smiling and cracking jokes*
*I wish you were here so that you could*
*See your daughter grow*
*But I know that things happen*
*I just wish it didn't happen to you*
*Or have to be you*
*Sometimes I question the world*

*and why it has to be so cold*
*And keep turning without you*
*And without me because sometimes*
*I'm not even here*
*I find my thoughts wherever you are*
*The way you left wasn't fair*
*But I hope you're amongst the stars*
*In the wind, protecting your mother,*
*Your family, and friends*
*I hope the heavens keep you safe*
*And your soul is at ease*
*And maybe, just maybe*
*I can find my peace*

## Do the angels cry

*I heard an angel cry out today*
*I think it heard my cry*
*It said "everything will be ok"*
*I said "I just don't understand why"*
*To which it replied "why what?"*
*"why do people have to die?"*
*The Angel began to weep a beautiful cry*
*It said "when people die, angels multiply"*

# There was a Kiana Rice

*Often times I think about death*
*And how someone once*
*Was alive and breathing*
*How someone once was...*
*Only to not be anymore*
*I think of their families*
*And the imprint they have left*
*On the ones that they love*
*And that loved them beyond life*
*Beyond the limits of the sky*
*I think about how they were real*
*And not in mentality*
*But physically*
*Its crazy how the rest of the world*
*Might not have ever known*
*That they existed*
*Or that they saw demise*
*They'll never know of their victories*
*Or of their cries*
*It's hard to explain my mind*
*But I think about these things*
*From time to time*
*I've lost people I loved*
*And my heart still aches*
*But someone somewhere else*
*Will never know my pain*
*They won't get to understand*
*How much that person meant to me*
*How much their voice resonates with*
*My soul*
*And how much it hurt for me to let go*
*I guess it's all just human nature*

*But it's a shame we don't get to experience*
*Each other's light while we're alive*
*So many have been wiped away*
*And over time their faces and voices*
*Start to fade*
*And the world around us will move on*
*And all we'll have is pictures in frames*
*But I don't want to be forgotten*
*I can imagine the dead would say the same*
*I love the people who love me*
*And I know the whole world won't get*
*To experience my light*
*But I want the world to know*
*That there was a Kiana Rice*
*And there was a you*
*And so on*
*And so forth.*

### In hopes that you'll understand

*Wish I could make it easy*
*Wish I could stop thinking*
*It's like I don't know how to do*
*Anything else*
*I can't make a decision for myself*
*It's hard to understand myself*
*It's really disappointing*
*To feel like you do nothing right*
*It's hard to put myself first*
*And even harder to put up a fight*
*I feel bad about everything*
*Even when it means doing*
*What I feel is best for me*
*Sometimes I feel like a bad person*
*And other times I don't feel present*
*Sometimes I get happy*
*And others I deal with depression*
*But don't get me wrong*
*I love life*
*It's just hard to explain the things*
*On my mind*
*I don't want to worry a soul*
*I know things will get better*
*And so I try to be strong*
*I feel like no one understands*
*But I know I'm not alone*
*I can't see a future*
*But I have faith that there is one*
*I feel out of place everyday*
*And never satisfied with anything*
*And I feel bad about it because*
*I'm so blessed*

*But this is my truth*
*The things I feel I can't say*
*And so I write it down in hopes*
*That you'll understand*

# *If I cried*

*If I cried know that I love you*
*For this is one of the things I hate the most*

# Healing...

*I've chosen to heal even if it kills me.*

# Hello, Goodbye

*Hello to new beginnings*
*Goodbye to staying the same*
*Goodbye to old habits*
*And hello to making a change*
*So many goodbyes and hellos*
*That it's almost insane*
*But without saying goodbye*
*They'll be no hellos to say*
*I used to think goodbyes were bitter*
*But goodbyes are so sweet*
*All things come and go*
*All things come to a cease*
*There is no bitterness in letting go*
*Only growth*
*Only more room to accept the hellos*

*Goodbye, Hello.*

## *New endings and new beginnings*

*God bless the new ends*
*The end of something that brought me*
*A new beginning*
*Because without them I wouldn't know*
*What I know now*
*I thought that the end of a lot of things*
*Would hurt but wow look how*
*They brought me something new*
*That I could be proud of*

## *Moving forward*

*Sometimes moving forward is hard*
*If you don't know what the future holds*
*But I will go before I stay in yesterday*
*Every day I learn a new lesson*
*New heartbreaks*
*And New pains*
*And although it never gets easy*
*I grow every new day*
*Sometimes the world feels too big*
*And I feel small*
*But I am large in spirit*
*In spirit I am tall*
*So I won't complain*
*I will move forward*
*Toward a better understanding of life*
*And I will fight for what I feel in my*
*Heart is right*
*And I will let go of things that bring me*
*Aches and pains*
*I will not live in fear of tomorrow*
*And I will not stand in anger and shame*
*Because life is not a burden*
*Life and love is a choice*
*So I choose to live and love*
*I will stand in love*
*And I will love like I've never been hurt*
*And I will love until I feel alright*
*And I will love until love brings me light*
*And I will keep moving forward until the*
*Day I die*

## Don't tell me I've changed

*Don't tell me i've changed*
*Because you've stayed the same*
*And I took the opportunity to grow*
*Don't tell me i've changed*
*Because you've been gone*
*Out of my life for so long*
*And I'm not the person*
*That you used to know*

### *It was nice to know you*

*It was nice to know you*
*But a new season has come*
*You have gone*
*And I have changed*
*Loving you was like finding loose change*
*All over the place and messy*
*But even love is not perfect*
*Even the blind can see who's worth it*
*And this Love was not*
*And in the midst of all that was lost*
*I have learned many of lessons*
*How to pay attention to signs*
*And not sleep on my blessings*
*You were a moment in time*
*A sublime of light in my life*
*When I needed it the most*
*And for that I am forever thankful*
*But you were not meant to walk*
*Forward with me*
*Your chapter ended long ago*
*So I stayed there refusing to turn pages*
*So that I could be with you*
*And now I realize that if I don't turn the page*
*I will never know a new chapter*
*And what is the point of reading if I*
*Can't finish the book?*
*And although this is how long it took*
*For me to realize,*
*it is better to know now*
*than to cry later*
*I wanted to hold you*
*There was so many things I wanted*

*To show you*
*And even though I can no longer*
*Grow with you*
*Through the good and the bad*
*It was nice to know you*

### *All the things that I have learned*

*I've learned not to paint a new picture*
*Once I've been showed true colors*
*I've learned that loving myself*
*And wanting to be loved back is not a burden*
*I've learned that love is a gamble*
*But that doesn't mean you shouldn't play*
*I've learned that two wrongs*
*don't make a right*
*And that I can't make people stay*
*I've learned that in life you*
*Have to compromise*
*Nobody is always right*
*I've learned that peace of mind*
*Is better than always putting up a fight*
*I've learned that lessons*
*Turn into blessings*
*As long as you learn from your past*
*Mistakes and correct them*
*I've learned that taking responsibility*
*Is better than blaming everyone else*
*I've learned that sometimes you have to let*
*Go of the people you love*
*And hope that they better themselves*
*I've learned that you have to love yourself*
*Before you can truly love someone else*
*I've learned that if you don't love yourself*
*No one else will*
*I've learned that hatred is for the broken*
*And forgiveness is for the healed*
*I've learned that love is not easy*
*But it should not be painful*
*I've learned that peace can be found in anything*

*As long as you believe that peace is attainable*
*I've learned that to achieve your goals*
*You have to believe that you're able*
*I've learned that self love is not easy*
*But all good things take time*
*I've learned that sometimes you have*
*To accept things for what they are*
*And hope everything turns out fine*
*I've learned that everyday is a new*
*opportunity to make a change*
*These are all of the things I've learned*
*And I'm still learning to this day*

## Growing apart

When two hearts grow apart
There's nothing really that you can do
You have to learn to deal with it
And do what's best for you
Sometimes things just don't work out
The relationship has clearly took
A turn for the worse
And sometimes you have to realize
That it's never going to work
All it's going to do is leave you in pain
Or make you hurt
So sometimes it's best for two hearts
To grow apart so they can both have a new start
And learn to trust and love again
And rebuild their broken hearts

## *Realization at 6:05 a.m.*

*I'm who I needed this whole time*
*I was trying to find me in you*
*When there was no you and I*
*This whole time*

## *Ok?*

*I got lost by myself*
*I didn't need your help*
*It wasn't love that drove*
*Me insane*
*Ok?*

## Don't go interrupting my peace

*Don't go interrupting my peace*
*For it is all that's left of me*
*I've spilled my feelings out on*
*Marble floors just for you to turn*
*Around and ignore me*
*I've picked myself up of the ground now*
*Step by step I've stood up*
*And all it took was you to turn your*
*Back on me and break my last straw*
*Broke each other's hearts last fall*
*But now I've come to see*
*That if you cannot love me*
*Don't go interrupting my peace*

## Heartless

*I thought I was heartless*
*But being heartless is not to feel*
*And I feel EVERYTHING*
*When the feelings are real*
*I feel everything until the hurt is healed*
*But I am stronger now so i've learned to deal*

## Good girls

*Everybody wants a good girl*
*But no one really wants a good girl*
*They'd rather have someone selfish*
*With no conscience*
*With no heart*
*With no mind*
*And a sunken soul*
*Good girls love you like*
*your heart is their own*
*Good girls are not easy to come by*
*So I see why you wouldn't know*
*A good girl if she were standing*
*Right in front of you*

*You say you want a good girl*
*But you don't want a girl who is*
*Good to herself*
*You don't want a girl who is strong*
*Or knows her worth*
*You want a girl who you can use*
*For emotional support*
*And then leave her when you find*
*What you believe is the next best thing*
*Your next little fling*
*Good girls got a lot more to offer than that*
*I think it scares you*
*Because you know you have to commit*
*And there's no way around it*

*You said you want a good girl*
*But you don't want to have to work to*
*Get to know her*
*Or to get close to her*

*You don't want to know the things about*
*Her that she holds in*
*You want a quick fix*
*You want someone stupid*
*But do you want to know the best thing*
*About good girls?*
*They remain good even when you've*
*Been bad to them*
*They do not seek revenge*
*Or wish hate on your life*
*They wish you blessings and move on*
*They wish you love and light*
*Good girls aren't a dime a dozen*
*And if you have one*
*I hope you realize*
*Before it's too late*
*Because treating a good girl bad*
*Has karma to pay*

## I'm not gonna let you

*I'm not gonna let you make me hate love*
*And all that comes with it*
*Just Because it didn't work*
*And I was hurt yet again*
*For the however many times*
*And I won't lie*
*Because for a second I convinced myself*
*That you were the only one out there*
*Made for me*
*But what I Couldn't see*
*Was that loving you at some point in time*
*Was like Loving a brick wall*
*Me talking to you and you not talking at all*
*But I deserve better and I know it*
*Sometimes it's just hard to let go of*
*What you know*
*Especially if you're not ready*
*For the person to go*

*But I've seem to come to my senses about it*
*You don't love me enough to change your ways*
*You've disappointed me yet again*
*And now I'm ashamed*
*Because I told everyone you were different*
*With stars in my eyes*
*Deep down I knew I was telling myself*
*And everyone else another lie*
*But was I lying if I really believed it?*
*I thought about the long term*
*But now I don't need it*
*For a second I couldn't believe it,*
*You let yourself slip away*

*For whatever reason*
*But this time you can stay gone*
*I'm not going to let you ruin my heart*
*When it's a space another man*
*That has the capacity to love me*
*Can call a home*

*And this time I won't pick up the phone*
*Letting you tell me things that make*
*Me believe that this time is different*
*Because the truth is that it isn't*
*You're the same that you've always been*
*You can't reciprocate the love*
*Because your heart is broken*
*But it was broken way before me*
*And I don't have the tools to fix it*
*And everything I said, I truly meant it*
*Didn't cost you a dime to love me*
*I wonder if you felt anything when*
*You we're putting everyone else above me*
*But now you've made your bed,*
*I hope you can lay in it*
*And I can't let you turn me cold*
*Because I don't deserve this*
*If it was worth it,*
*You would fight for it like I do*
*I don't even wonder if you really cared*
*Anymore because it's apparent*
*that you don't care enough*
*And as hard as it is*
*I'm not gonna let you*
*Make me hate love*

## *Heart of steel*

*My heart don't break*
*My heart don't crease*
*My heart don't lie*
*My love don't cease*
*My heart ain't perfect*
*But my heart is real*
*My heart ain't glass*
*My heart's made of steel*
*Still follow my heart*
*While they follow their legs*
*Still working on me*
*While they watch*
*And judge instead*
*My hearts very alive*
*My heart ain't dead*
*My heart pump life*
*My hearts just fine*
*My heart ain't perfect*
*But it heals with time*

## Leo

*I was built with strength in my bones*
*And pride strong like a lion's*
*I walk to the beat of my own drum*
*And never wanted to be a follower*
*A natural born leader*
*Even when it wasn't cool to lead*
*I'd rather be an outcast*
*Than follow like a sheep*
*I was born a Leo*
*A warrior*

# I just want to see you happy

*I just want to see you happy*
*Haven't you been sad enough*
*I know times get lonely*
*I know that life is rough*
*I know you've been feeling numb*
*And trying your hardest to heal*
*I know it's easier said than done*
*I know it hurts to feel*
*But you've been down long enough*
*I want to see you up*
*Please don't give up*
*You'll have another chance*
*To forget today's sorrow*
*And start again tomorrow*
*I know it sounds cliche*
*But I just want to see you happy*

## It's a shame we change/f*ck the world

It's a shame we change
For people who will never appreciate us
It's a shame we change for strangers
Who haven't walked a mile in our shoes
Even if we do change for them
We won't be happy with ourselves
And in the end we still lose
So you choose
You or the World?
Because only one can win
Only one can get by
I say fuck the world
Because all you get is one life
I say fuck the world
They don't live in your mind
They haven't seen life with your eyes
They haven't loved with your heart
They haven't seen your potential or drive
Your will to do right
It's a shame we change
Just to change their minds
So I say fuck the world
They haven't lived my life

## In the garden where the flowers grow

*In the garden where the flowers grow*
*I've come to know a love unfamiliar*
*A love that comes from within*
*That set me on fire*
*A feeling that's grown higher and higher*
*In the depths of my heart*
*A love that brought the passion*
*In me out of the dark*
*This was a love you couldn't give me*
*Even if your heart directed you to*
*A love that i'd been missing for what*
*Felt like a lifetime*
*I felt like you were my lifeline until*
*I opened my eyes and now I can*
*Never turn back*
*This love came with everything you lacked*
*I was lost in my mind without it*
*I couldn't see the good in me*
*But all the wicked around me*
*All the things i'm not proud of*
*But this love I will not take for granted*
*I took a trip to the garden where the*
*Flowers grow and now I know*
*Self love*

## ?

*I don't know where I'm going*
*But I'm going*
*I don't know how I'll get there*
*But I'll get there*
*I don't know how I'll stay strong*
*But I'll stay strong*
*I know that wrong ain't always right*
*And right ain't always wrong*
*I know it ain't easy to feel alone*
*I know it's hard to walk by faith*
*If your sight isn't strong*
*But still we walk by faith and carry on*

## Pretty hearts

*God bless the pretty hearts*
*In a world full of ugly*
*In a volatile state*
*Hearts so full of love*
*That they drown out all the hate*
*God bless the pretty hearts*
*And their willingness to forgive*
*Even after all the darkness*
*That they've experienced*
*God bless the pretty hearts*
*The ones that have been*
*Broken and used*
*But decided not to destroy*
*Other hearts*
*Because they know what that pain*
*Could do*
*God bless the pretty hearts*
*That have never folded*
*under pressure*
*But fought against their skeletons*
*And made it through*
*The stormy weather*

## *Audacity*

*Oh how I have the audacity to love*
*After my heart has been walked*
*All over and crushed*
*Some say that it's dumb*
*To continue giving out love*
*After you've been broken*
*They say it's better to be numb*
*And I won't lie because*
*I believe them sometimes*
*But I owe it to myself to not give up*
*Oh how I have the audacity to feel*
*When people's feelings towards*
*Me have not been real*
*Some say that I'm a fool*
*To allow myself to feel feelings*
*After I've been used*
*They say it's better to be cold*
*And I won't lie because*
*I believe them sometimes*
*But I owe it to myself to be bold*
*With how I feel*

*The audacity to heal*

## Horizon

*I am 6ft deep*
*In things I cannot control*
*How it got this far?*
*I really don't know*
*Sometimes I forget that there's a surface*
*And so I stay below*
*And before I know it*
*I'm stuck in limbo*
*All things cannot be explained*
*And how I feel will not always make sense*
*But if I chose to not dig my way out*
*I'll be trapped under the cement*
*It hasn't always been this hard to live*
*It's always been hard to vent*
*But I have to survive*
*Because it was meant*
*It was my destiny long before*
*Life was breathed into me*
*To see the horizon*

# Drowning

Drowning
Not literally but metaphorically
As humans we drown everyday
I want to be drowned in love
Drowned me in faith
Drown my demons
And drown my hate
Drown this poem
After you read what I have to say
Because floating is hard if
You don't know how
And sinking is all too easy
And living is all too hard
But still we keep on breathing
Ain't no use in drowning in sorrow
When you'll wake up tomorrow
And the clouds will be white
And the trees will be green
And the sky will still be blue
And the sun will still sprinkle
Down on you
You may have drowned yesterday
But today is new
So stop drowning yourself
In the things you cannot change
And pray for the ones who don't
Think they deserve to see another day
And don't judge others
For what you do not understand
Because they cannot drown
If you help them stand

*And if you're drowning right now*
*Keep your hope alive*
*We've all drowned before*
*But we didn't die*

# Healing

*In the wake of the storm*
*I open my eyes*
*Only to be left in rubble*
*And as if there's no trouble*
*I stay and lay there*
*And I won't get up even*
*If the earth crumbles*
*Because I wallow in self pity*
*As if there's no tomorrow*
*All I wanted was to be good*
*I wanted the world to love me*
*And if I was done wrong*
*I let it burn me*
*Because If I lived in the previous hurt*
*I eliminated the chance of being*
*Hurt again*
*I'm aware that I gain nothing*
*From living in my pain and misfortune*
*But like a drug I revisited it*
*Time and time again*
*Until one day I wanted to heal*
*Even if it killed me*
*And that's the beauty of it all*
*All things bitter sweet*
*Healing is not beautiful*
*Nor is it painless and easy*
*But healing is better than feeling*
*Like you can't continue*
*And all your issues are permanent*
*Because they are not*
*And though we cannot turn*
*Back the clock*

*You can not refuse to heal*
*Damaged souls do not have an easy role*
*In a world full of ugly and hate*
*But if you decide not to be here today*
*How will you know what new feelings*
*And healings tomorrow could bring?*

## What a life

In this life of mine
I've rose to find hardships
But in the midst of it I have
Also grown to know peace
Pain once whittled me
And turned me into a mere
Shell of myself
I watched myself scream
And gasp for help from the inside
But on the outside I did
Not say a peep
Sleep could not expel me
From my living nightmare
It could not relieve the grief
In my heart
This life of mine was the abyss
A total eclipse
Crippling dark
Until my eyes were opened
By the most high
And I was lifted from the dirt
Darkness poured out of my heart
Like black coffee out of a hollow mug
And I was filled with life again
All of my sins covered in the blood
Of Jesus
and as if that wasn't enough
I could breathe again

# Love...

I love love, and I hope love loves me.

## *If you want to love someone like me*

*If you want to love*
*Someone like me be prepared*
*For what it's going to do to you*

## Me & Love

Me and love are not strangers
We've danced with danger many times
We've dealt with anger more times
Then I care to count
Me and love
Are always up
Until we're right back down
Always taken in circles
Round and round
And then left to pick up
The pieces when no one's around
Me & love are beautiful when we're happy
A mistake when I'm sad
But love is naive
And i've gone mad
But i've grown up
Love has not
Love loves with blind eyes
And love has costs
I have a hard time trusting love
But love embraces me with open arms
And when things get tough
And we're left all alone
Love leans on me
And I lean on love

Me & Love

## *We don't plan to fall*

*Sometimes we don't plan to fall*
*In love or like someone*
*But I guess sometimes the*
*Stars just align that way*
*I never thought about*
*Anything like this and*
*I know that sounds crazy*
*To say*

## Soulmate

*Are you out there looking for me*
*Like I'm looking for you?*
*Are you out there getting your heart broken*
*By girls who don't love you for you*
*Out there searching for what you're missing*
*Who you should be kissing*
*And giving your all to*
*I'm that girl that God put on this earth*
*Just for you*
*Your soulmate*
*The one who you'll go on a long journey to find*
*As I will for you*
*We don't know each other now*
*But soon we'll intertwine*
*And when we do we'll find*
*That we didn't really know*
*Love at all before each other*
*Everyone else was practice*
*For that very moment when we lock eyes*
*And our souls touch each other in places that hands cannot meet*
*And in that moment we'll be*
*Like stars dancing with each other*
*In the pitch black of night*
*And though we won't have everything*
*We will be just fine*
*Because we'll have each other*
*And there won't be another you or I*
*Like roots of a tree*
*You are rooted in me*
*Our souls are tied*
*Like shoelaces*
*With many knots in them*
*I will give your heart the healing it needs*

## Next lover

Please let my next lover be patient
And in tune with his heart
Let him be honest and real from the start
Please let him be gentle and kind
Please let him be a thinker
Who takes pride in his mind
Please let him care less about the physical
And more about what I think
Let him be brave and be a man who prays
Let him walk with a purpose like a King
Please let him be confident
Because he knows what he brings
Let him mean what he says and
Say what he means
Please let him love me for me
Let him be wise and understanding of life
Let him be someone who can
Put his pride aside
Please let him be my other half
Someone I can rely on
And a shoulder to cry on
Someone who will listen to my crazy
Thoughts and ideas as if they were his own
Let him be someone that feels like home
Let him be a lover and not a fighter
I'm tired of fighting with people I love
Let him understand I'm here to love him
And not to judge
Please let him be sent by God to me
Let him know that I'll be all he needs
If he puts his trust in me
I pray that he's understanding

*and soft spoken*
*I pray that we both can be open*
*Please let him know that I am waiting*
*And I am patient*
*And loving*
*And honest*
*And ready*
*For my next lover*

## *Someone to love me*

*I want someone to love me like*
*I love them for once*
*Because I'm at tired of being tired of love*
*I just want to feel good about somebody*
*without worrying if they feel the same*
*Someone to love me like I love the rain*
*Someone who will stick around through all the pain*
*And even though I can't give them the world*
*Their love will still remain*
*I just want to lay down at night and*
*Thank God for blessing me with the kind of love*
*That puts the stars to shame*
*I just want to feel butterflies every time*
*I hear their name*
*I don't want to be clueless and confused*
*I don't want to be mistreated and used*
*I want to learn to trust again*

## *Let me know*

*I don't know what to make of this*
*I don't know how you feel*
*Sometimes I feel like I can read you*
*And other times I have no clue*
*What you're thinking*
*Do I stay on your mind*
*Like you stay on mine?*
*Am I moving too fast*
*Or am I moving to slow*
*I need you to let me know*

## Do I?

*People ask me do I love you*
*And I can't help but blush*
*Maybe I'm just in love*
*With the thought of love*
*Even though I'm not*

## Is it love?

*Is it love that I am missing*
*In the depths of my soul*
*I thought it would be alright*
*If I'd just let myself go*
*But I am afraid of the unknown*
*And therefore I cannot blow*
*This here out of proportion*
*Is it love, is it love, is it love*
*I hope it is*
*Because if it isn't this is*
*Just another poem*
*Without any real meaning*
*I thought if I got into the lines*
*That I could read between them*
*But I'm not that good at telling*
*Things apart so I don't know*
*If it is love that is coming from*
*My heart*
*Is it love*
*Or is it exactly what it isn't*

# I dream of..

*I dream of holding you*
*As you lay on my chest*
*Listening to my heart beat*
*While I rub your hair and*
*Your eyes roll back as you fall asleep*
*I lay there listening to you breathe*
*As my heart races*
*Making the butterflies*
*In my stomach rise to occasion*

### Just us two

*I wish the world would be still*
*So I can walk with you a little longer*
*And tell you what you mean to me*

## Love

*I want to love and be loved*
*For reasons deeper than skin*
*I am capable of love and compassion*
*Things that come from within*

## The life of roses

*Our love is like roses*
*Delicate and fragile*
*But beautiful in every*
*Sense of the word*
*And though roses*
*Die within time*
*This will never burn*
*I think of all the*
*Moments where the*
*Rest of the world was*
*At ease around you and I*
*And it was just us two*
*Me and you*
*Lovers*
*Connected by*
*The grace of God*
*And an alignment of stars*
*And here we are*

## What it's like to love someone like you

Sometimes it's trying
But I had to learn that these
Kind of things take time
You're one of the best
Things in my life & I'm proud
To call you mines
We're not perfect together
But that's what makes us real
We each have parts of us
That we have to learn to heal
But I'm ok with that
and you're ok with it too
I couldn't imagine a world
Without you
Even if we don't end up
Together
I'm happy with the time spent
I know not everything lasts
Forever but at least I hope
This could be it
And we could be together
For a long time
Raise kids together and
Live the good life
Being with you, the options
Are endless
And thoughts of our future
Stay heavy on my mind
But for now in the present
I am yours and you are mines
You make me laugh
You make me mad

*You make me sad*
*You make me glad*
*There's not a time I don't*
*Wish to spend with you*
*There's always a time*
*I wish I had*
*I hope you know how*
*Much I love you*
*What I would do for you*
*And I know you feel the*
*Same way too*
*There's a million reasons*
*For the way I feel*
*But these are a few*
*About what's it's like to*
*Love someone like you*

## *Unconditionally*

*I love you unconditionally*
*For my love is without conditions*
*I don't need a thing from you*
*But love*

## *You.*

*I wish the world really knew you,*
*Like really knew you*
*So they could see exactly what I see*
*Sometimes I wonder if I really know you,*
*Like really know you*
*You're really good at hiding your pain*
*But I love you like I have nothing to lose*
*And everything to gain*
*I wish you could see what I see in you*
*You have so much potential*
*There's not a thing in this world*
*I don't believe you couldn't do*
*I hope you achieve all of your dreams*
*I hope one day you'll feel complete*
*I love how you love me*
*Even when I'm annoying*
*And even when I'm mean*
*I pray for us to learn how to love*
*Each other completely*
*Even the things we do not like*
*I pray that we grow together*
*And learn to do things right*
*I try not to be afraid of the future*
*But I hope that you'll remain in my life*
*Because I am in love with you*
*When I'm with you I do not watch the time*
*I'm just in the moment*
*And I hope this moment will always last*
*When I'm around you I don't think*
*About my problems and pain*
*I think it's safe to say you're my other half*
*This love is unconditional*

*It is Without limits*
*I couldn't imagine a world without*
*You in it.*

***I love you***

## *A love like the sun*

*I want a love like the sun*
*One that warms the outside of*
*My body when the inside feels cold*
*I want a love that makes me feel like gold*
*Like the sun is always shining*
*I want a love that makes me glow*
*I want a love that is good to me*
*And helps me grow*
*I want a love that will still shine*
*Even when there's snow*
*I want a love that feels like picnics*
*And star filled nights*
*I want a love that feels right*
*I want a love that loves me back*
*Like the sun loves my skin*
*I want a love that pulls me closer*
*And always wants to hold my hands*
*I want a loved that is beautiful like the*
*Clear blue sky I lay under*
*I want a love that feels like summer*
*I want a love that makes me get out of bed*
*And out of my head*
*Because I stay there too much*
*I want a love that smiles back at me*
*A love like the sun*

# Open

Open books get all the looks
A closed book could never get
A closed book don't want to be
Closed but people rarely try to
Open it

An open book is brave but a
Closed book hasn't figured out
How to turn a page
Yet

Open books open all closets
And skeletons climb out their graves
Maybe a closed book is afraid
Of what might come to the light
An open book is easy to read
But a closed book is worth the fight

Who's to say an open book is a good
Thing and just because a book is open
Does not mean it holds substance
Filled things & by all means
You can applaud an open book
But if you haven't opened the closed
Book one day you should have a look

And you might be shocked to find
That the closed book was open all
This time just waiting for someone
Who would try to understand
All of the madness written inside

Printed in the United States
By Bookmasters